A GIFT FOR:

....

FROM:

....

Life Is...

Just
Better

...with Jesus

ANNE GRAHAM LOTZ

COUNTRYMAN
®

Published by J. Countryman, a division of Thomas Nelson, Inc, Nashville, Tennessee 37214.

Published in association with the literary agency of Alive Communications, Inc., 7680 Goddard Street, Suite 200, Colorado Springs, CO 80920.

Compiled and edited by Terri Gibbs

All Scripture quotations, unless otherwise indicated, are taken from the Holy Bible, New International Version. Copyright ©1973 International Bible Society. Used by permission of Zondervan Bible Publisher.

Other Scripture references are from the following sources: The King James Version (KJV) of the Bible.

The New King James Version (NKJV®), copyright 1979, 1980, 1982, Thomas Nelson, Inc., Publishers. Used by permission.

Designed by The DesignWorks Group, Sisters, Oregon.

ISBN 13: 978-1-4041-0399-6

www.thomasnelson.com
www.jcountryman.com

Printed and bound in China

Contents

Preface 7

I. Jesus Is the Savior Who Has Redeemed Us.......11

Jesus Sustains My Life.........13

Jesus Is Our Way Home 15

Jesus—It's Still His Cross....17

Jesus Brings New Life 19

Jesus Brings Life from Death.21

Jesus Is My Life 23

Jesus Invites Me to Follow ..25

Jesus Is God's Blessing.........27

Jesus Restores Me on the Inside............................29

Jesus Forgives Me of My Sin .31

Jesus Invites Me to Come ...33

Jesus Gives Me Access to God................................35

Jesus Opens My Ears to God's Word 37

Jesus Is Revealed in Me.......39

Jesus Is Thinking of Me......41

II. Jesus Is the Son of God Who Has Freed Us 43

Jesus Is Molding Me 45

Jesus Is the Source of My Life...............................47

Jesus Enlarges My Life 49

Jesus Answers—When I Ask..51

Jesus Knows Me..................53

Jesus Makes Me Clean 55

Jesus Satisfies 57

Jesus Showers Me with Blessings 59

Jesus Cares About Me.........61

Jesus Helps Me Forgive Others 63

Jesus Makes a Little Bit, Enough................................65

Jesus Gives Me His Undivided Attention 67

Jesus Gives Me the Comforter..69

Jesus Opens My Mind to His Word........................71

III. JESUS IS THE SHEPHERD WHO GUIDES US 73

Jesus Reveals God's Love 75

Jesus Is God in the Flesh.....77

Jesus Does Care 79

Jesus Is Trustworthy 81

Jesus Is Everywhere 83

Jesus Is with Me in Suffering 85

Jesus Is My Shepherd 87

Jesus Helps Me Soar 89

Jesus Answers Prayer 91

Jesus Guarantees Immediate Access to God 93

Jesus Is God's Ultimate Answer.................................95

Jesus Is My Personal Friend 97

Jesus Weeps with Me 99

Jesus Empowers Me 101

Jesus Fills Me with God's Love 103

Jesus Defeats Fear 105

Jesus Is My Antidote to Fear 107

IV. JESUS IS THE ETERNAL KING WHO LOVES US ..109

Jesus Loves Me..................111

Jesus Is Fully Present with Me 113

Jesus Rewards Me 115

Jesus Promises Me Eternal Life 117

Jesus Will Honor Me 119

Jesus Is Preparing Heaven for Me 121

Jesus Will Take Me Home ..123

Acknowledgments 126

Jesus is the most important Man, not just in our nation, not just on planet earth, but in the entire universe! And He isn't important just for four years or eight years, but forever and ever and ever! Furthermore, the most important Man in the universe thinks I am so important, He gave His own life for me! How can I feel depressed by the smallness of my life when the most important Man in the universe died for me, rules over me now, and will one day return for me? In the eyes of the Lord Jesus Christ, I am important. My life has value.

No only does my life have value but in every way imaginable it is better with Jesus. He not only gives meaning and purpose to life, He gives direction and makes a difference in life. If you are depressed by the smallness of your life, you can find encouragement through Jesus! If you are defeated by life, you can find hope through Jesus.

Jesus is our provider, our strength, our help . . .
when we struggle with sin . . .
when we are inconsistent in commitment . . .
when we stumble and fall . . .
when we falter and fail . . .
when we are tried and tempted.

He is the Savior Who has redeemed us,
the Son of God Who has freed us,
the Shepherd Who guides us,
the Eternal King who loves us.

He is the foundation on which we build our lives . . .
the Rock on which we stand.

His faithfulness is new every morning and fresh
every evening.

Eternity will not be enough time to thank Him for
Who He is and what He has done—for you—and for me.

Anne Graham Lotz

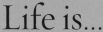

Life is...

Just

Better

...with Jesus

"I have come that they might have life,
and have it to the full."

JOHN 10:10

PART ONE

Jesus

Is the Savior Who Has Redeemed Us

He has the
power to
create and sustain
the universe.

Jesus SUSTAINS MY LIFE

*The Spirit of God has made me,
and the breath of the Almighty gives me life.*

JOB 33:4 NKJV

T hink about it for a moment!

Our planet is ninety-three million miles away from the sun. If the sun were any closer to earth, we would burn up. If it were any farther away from earth, we would freeze.

Our planet tilts exactly 23 degrees on its axis, giving us four seasons a year. If it tilted at any other angle, we would have massive continents of ice.

The moon is the exact distance from earth to give us two ocean tides a day. If it were any greater or lesser distance, the earth would be flooded.

The ocean floor is at an exact depth that gives us oxygen, which sustains human life. If the depth were any different, the air we breathe would be poisonous.

The atmosphere is the exact density to keep meteors and space objects from hitting us. If it were any thinner, we would be constantly bombarded by objects from outer space.

And Who keeps all this in perfect order? Who keeps Earth from getting sucked into some gigantic black hole, or planets from spinning out of control, or stars from falling from the sky? The answer is none other than Jesus—the Living Logos. If He has the power to create and sustain the universe, how can you think His power is insufficient for you?

JUST GIVE ME JESUS

"*I am the way, the truth, and the life. No one comes to the Father except through Me.*"

John 14:6 NKJV

Jesus Is Our Way Home

*There is no other name under heaven given
among men by which we must be saved.*

ACTS 4:12 NKJV

O ther religions and peoples may have some truth,
but only Jesus Christ is *the* Truth for everyone who
has ever been born into the human race, regardless
of culture, age, nationality, generation, heritage, gender,
color, or language. Jesus said that He Himself is the only
Way to get to heaven! We must come to God through Him
or we don't come at all.

During the Vietnam War, a story was reported about a
paratrooper who had been air-dropped into the jungle and
couldn't find his way out. A native guide had to be sent into
the jungle to find the lost man then lead him safely to his
base. The guide became the man's way to safety—his "way
home." In the same manner, Jesus is "God's Guide," heaven-
dropped into the world to lead lost sinners safely "Home."
It stands to reason that if you refuse to acknowledge that
you are "lost," then you will not accept God's Way home.
But for those of us who know we have been lost, our
overwhelming gratitude for the Guide is enough to compel
us to tell others about Him—about the truth of their lost
condition and the truth about the Way out.

MY HEART'S CRY

There is
no other way
for you and me
to be saved.-

Jesus—It's Still His Cross

*In Him we have redemption through His blood,
the forgiveness of sins, according to the riches of His grace.*

EPHESIANS 1:7 NKJV

T he obedience of Jesus to His Father caused Him to lay down His life for you and me.

It was at the cross that God's curse for Adam's sin was coiled into a crown that Jesus wore.

It was at the cross that redemption was purchased for every believer by the sacrifice of God's Lamb.

It was at the cross that even the vilest offenders received, by faith, a full pardon for their sins.

It was at the cross that God's grace was poured out as a fountain filled with His own blood.

It was at the cross that the omnipotent Creator died for the human creature's sin.

And it's still at the cross of Jesus Christ where millions of men and women throughout the ages have laid down all that they are and all that they have as a debt of love to the One Who died for them. There is no other way for you and me to be saved from hell . . . to have our sins forgiven . . . to be reconciled to God . . . to receive eternal life . . . to go to heaven when we die, except through the cross.

MY HEART'S CRY

He who has the Son
has life.

1 John 3:12

Jesus BRINGS NEW LIFE

"Most assuredly, I say to you, he who hears My word and believes in Him who sent Me has everlasting life, and shall not come into judgment, but has passed from death into life."

JOHN 5:24 NKJV

Some time ago I attended one of my father's evangelistic crusades. When the invitation was given to the audience members to come to the platform in order to receive Jesus Christ as Savior and Lord, thousands of people responded by pouring down from the stadium seats onto the football field. Within a few moments the entire field was jammed with people who were spiritually being raised from the dead as they placed their faith in Christ. When I leaned over to comment on the scene to my husband, who was sitting with me, I saw tears streaming down his cheeks! And as I focused on others around me, beside and behind me, I saw one friend after another with tears running down his or her face—tears of sheer joy for those who were walking from darkness into the light and passing from death to life!

MY HEART'S CRY

We fix our eyes
not on what is seen,
but on what is unseen.

2 Corinthians 4:18

Jesus BRINGS LIFE
FROM DEATH

When He had given thanks, He broke it
and said, "Take, eat; this is My body which is broken
for you; do this in remembrance of Me."

1 CORINTHIANS 11:24 NKJV

I t was not on the throne of world rulership that Jesus came into power, as the disciples had imagined, but it was on the cross where He was broken. Like the grain of wheat, He had to die in order to be raised up with the power to reproduce His life hundreds of thousands of times over—in the lives of you and me and believers all through the centuries.

Every time we take Holy Communion in our churches, isn't this one of the reasons we remember His death with such gratitude? As we eat the bread, are we not thanking Him for His body that was broken? As we drink the cup, are we not thanking Him for His life that was not only poured out but raised up to give us eternal life? The only reason you and I are spiritually alive is because He died!

MY HEART'S CRY

To think of living even
one moment without
Jesus, of ever being
separated from Him,
is unthinkable!

Jesus Is My Life

You were bought at a price; therefore
glorify God in your body and in your spirit, which are God's.

1 CORINTHIANS 6:20 NKJV

ou and I were created for the purpose of glorifying God through the Christlike character of our lives and through the eternal fruitfulness of our service. When I get to heaven, I want to find that I fulfilled the potential of God's purpose for my life. I want Him to find pleasure in my birth and joy in my rebirth. I want Him to be confirmed that creating me was eternally worth it! For these "wants" to be realized then, I have to focus my entire life on His purpose now—which is what Jesus did.

If you and I are able to finish God's work, it will not be an accident. It will be because we have been focused every minute of every day of every week of every month of every year of our lives on God's purpose. And that purpose determines the way we manage our time, our money, our priorities, our relationships, our careers, and every other aspect of our lives. God is not something we add to our lives—He *is* our life! And our life's work!

To know God is to love God.

To love God is to serve God.

To serve God is to know Him better.

To know Him better is to love Him more.

To love Him more is to serve Him even more . . .

as increasingly we line up with His unique plan and purpose for our lives.

MY HEART'S CRY

23

*He alone is
my rock
and my salvation.*

Psalm 62:2

Jesus Invites Me to Follow

> *"If anyone desires to come after Me, let him deny himself, and take up his cross, and follow Me.*
>
> MATTHEW 16:24 NKJV

A s I go through life, sometimes my eyes involuntarily dart to people in front of me—on the TV screen I am watching, or on the pages of the newspaper or magazine I am reading, or in an audience to which I am speaking. And just for a moment, as I contemplate the accomplishments of someone else, I wonder, What if . . . ? Almost immediately I am reminded that I have a unique purpose in life that God has given me. Because Jesus invites me to follow Him.

To work out that purpose requires hours spent in reading and studying His Word as well as in meditating on how it applies to me. I then have to work out on the anvil of my own experience what His Word has said, which involves obedience, service, and sacrifice. I don't obey Him, or serve Him, or sacrifice for Him because I have to, but because I want to know Him, and that's the avenue He's laid out before me. With all my heart, I am just following Jesus. As a result, I am blessed with a deep sense of fulfillment and satisfaction and eternal significance, as well as with His presence in my life.

MY HEART'S CRY

*No matter now many
promises God has made,
they are "Yes" in Christ.*

2 Corinthians 1:20

Jesus Is God's Blessing

Honor and majesty You have placed upon him.
For You have made him most blessed forever;
You have made him exceedingly glad with Your presence.

PSALM 21:5–6 NKJV

J esus is our risen Lord and reigning King!

We are not our own.

We belong to Him.

Our lives no longer are to be lived according to what we *want* but according to what He *says*. We are His faithful servants.

The blessing He wants to pour out on your life and mine is not necessarily increased wealth or problem-free health or material prosperity. And it is not obtainable by prayerfully reciting a formula as though you are rubbing Aladdin's lamp, waiting for the Divine Genie to pop out and grant your request. The fullness of the blessing God wants to give you and me can be summed up in one word—Jesus! And if we want more blessing, then what we are really asking for is more of Jesus.

MY HEART'S CRY

Jesus offers us ample resources, but we have to receive them from Him in order to impart them to others.

Jesus Restores Me
on the Inside

The LORD is my shepherd; I shall not want.
He makes me to lie down in green pastures;
He leads me beside the still waters.

PSALM 23:2 NKJV

s "Jesus went up on a mountainside and sat down with his disciples" (John 6:3) they must have collapsed on a carpet of green grass covered with multicolored wildflowers. The snowcapped peak of Mount Hermon would have provided a dramatic backdrop while the glassy blue Sea of Galilee stretched out to the horizon in the spectacular foreground. Their weary, parched spirits must have drunk in the serene beauty like men coming out of a sun-scorched desert who thirstily guzzle water.

As Jesus and His disciples rested together on the mountainside, we have the beautiful picture of the Good Shepherd, making His sheep lie down in green pastures, leading them beside the still waters, that He might restore them on the inside. Jesus knew the demands that would be made on the disciples and Himself that very day, and He knew in order to meet those demands, they had to have some time alone together.

JUST GIVE ME JESUS

*Only God in
Christ has the power
to forgive sin.*

Jesus FORGIVES ME OF MY SIN

He who covers his sins will not prosper,
but whoever confesses and forsakes them will have mercy.

PROVERBS 28:13 NKJV

G od promises, "If we confess our sins, he is faithful and just and will forgive us our sins and purify us from all unrighteousness" (1 John 1:9). That word *confess* means to call sin by the same names that God does, to agree with God about your sin.

You and I often play games with the names we call sin to make it seem less like sin. For example,

We call the sin of unbelief, worry.

We call the sin of lying, exaggeration.

We call the sin of fornication, safe sex.

We call the sin of homosexuality, gay.

We call the sin of murder, the right to choose.

As long as we switch the labels on sin to make it seem less serious, we're being dishonest with ourselves and with God, and we remain unforgiven. But, if we say the same thing about our sin that God says—if we say, "God, it's lying. It's jealousy. It's lust. It's revenge. It's hate. It's adultery. It's unforgiveness"—God will forgive us! It doesn't matter how big the sin is or how small, it doesn't matter how long ago it was committed or how recently, it doesn't matter whether it was spontaneous or malicious. God will forgive you if you come to Him and confess your sin!

JUST GIVE ME JESUS

*In repentance and
rest is your salvation,
in quietness and trust
is your strength.*

ISAIAH 30:15

Jesus INVITES ME TO COME

*We have seen and testify that the
Father has sent the Son as Savior of the world.*

1 JOHN 4:14 NKJV

Our entrance into God's presence is not based on our own worthiness but on the worthiness of Jesus Christ! When we enter God's presence in Jesus' name, we are as accepted by God as Jesus is, because God counts us as His own dear children!

For a child, there is no place quite so safe and secure as within the father's arms. Jesus invites you and me, in His name, to come into His Father's presence through prayer, crawl up into His lap by faith, put our head on His shoulder of strength, feel His loving arms of protection around us, call Him "Abba" Daddy, and pour out our hearts to Him.

MY HEART'S CRY

"Ask and you will receive, and your joy will be complete."

John 16:24

Jesus GIVES ME ACCESS TO GOD

*Christ Jesus, who died—more than that, who was raised to life—
is at the right hand of God and is also interceding for us.*

ROMANS 8:34

When we come to God through prayer believing in Jesus' name, we enter into a world of privilege!

Doors open,

angels attend,

mountains move,

doubts disappear,

fears fade,

and the God of the universe bends down to hear what we have to say!

And He answers! What a privilege!

We don't have to go through a priest.

We don't have to go through a secretary.

We don't have to go to a temple.

We don't have to make a donation.

We don't have to go to a church building.

We don't have to come from the "right side of the tracks."

We don't have to use grammatically correct words.

Prayer is as simple as talking to God in Jesus' name.

MY HEART'S CRY

There is life-giving
power in
the Word of God!

Jesus Opens My Ears to God's Word

He wakens me morning by morning,
wakens my ear to listen like one being taught.

Isaiah 50:4

A t the most difficult times in my life—the loss of a baby, the forced removal from a church, the execution of a friend, the robbery of our home—God's Word has sustained me. There have been times when I have only been capable of reading a few verses at a time, yet the supernatural life-giving power of the Word of God has not only helped me maintain my emotional and mental balance, it has given me strength to go on, even if only one day at a time.

There is strength . . .

There is peace . . .

There is hope . . .

There is power . . .

There is life . . . in God's Word!

THE VISION OF HIS GLORY

*He has made
everything beautiful
in its time.*

ECCLESIASTES 3:11

Jesus Is Revealed in Me

The fruit of the Spirit is love, joy, peace, longsuffering, kindness, goodness, faithfulness, gentleness, self-control.

Galatians 5:22–23

T he revelation of the glory, or character, of Jesus Christ in our lives is often produced only through pressure and pain, stress and suffering. This principle came to mind when a friend was telling me about a gift he received at Christmas. It was a box with lots of little compartments, each one filled with different flavored tea bags. The compartments were labeled, but the tea bags were not. Shortly after the holidays, he got up early one morning, relishing the idea of a hot cup of tea. As he reached up on the shelf to grasp the box, it slipped out of his hands. In dismayed consternation, he looked at the tea bags that were scattered across his kitchen floor. Since they were no longer organized in the tidy little labeled compartments, he had no idea which tea bag was Earl Grey, which one was lemon mint, which one was Darjeeling, which one was herbal raspberry, or which one was green tea.

He gathered all the bags together and placed them in a plastic container. My friend related that from that day on, every morning was an adventure as he took out a tea bag at random, not knowing what flavor he had chosen until he plunged it into the boiling hot water. The heat of the water drew out the flavor of the tea bag.

Has God turned up the heat in your life? Could it be that this is your opportunity for God to glorify you as He uses the heat to conform you into the image of His Son? Is this your opportunity to glorify Him as the "heat" draws out the real flavor of your character, and Jesus is revealed through your love, joy, peace, patience, kindness, goodness, faithfulness, gentleness, and self-control?

My Heart's Cry

Jesus Is Thinking of Me

> *"I am the Alpha and the Omega," says the Lord God,*
> *"who is, and who was, and who is to come, the Almighty."*
>
> REVELATION 1:8

T he Alpha and the Omega" is a title that describes the eternal omniscience of Jesus Christ. The *alpha* is the first letter and the *omega* is the last letter in the Greek alphabet. Through the alphabet all of our words, all of our wisdom, and all of our knowledge are expressed. Jesus is the beginning and end of the alphabet, the summation of all wisdom and knowledge.

What does the omniscience of Christ mean to me personally? It means I have always been on His mind. Think of it: The most important Man in the universe has always been thinking of me! Wonder of wonders! I have never been out of His thoughts! Even as He hung on the cross, He was thinking of me by name! Dying for me by name! And when He was raised from the dead on that first Easter Sunday, He was raised with me on His mind!

THE VISION OF HIS GLORY

PART TWO

Jesus

IS THE SON OF GOD
WHO HAS FREED US

Like clay in the hand
of the potter,
so are you in my hand.

JEREMIAH 18:6

Jesus Is Molding Me

*O Lord, You are our Father; we are the clay,
and You our potter; and all we are the work of Your hand.*

Isaiah 64:8 nkjv

As the Potter, Jesus uses suffering as the pressure on the wet "clay" of our lives. Under His gentle, loving touch, our lives are molded into a "shape" that pleases Him. But the shape that is so skillfully wrought is not enough. He not only desires our lives to be useful, but He also wants our character to be radiant. And so He places us in the furnace of affliction until our "colors" are revealed—colors that reflect the beauty of His own character.

Without the preparation of the loving, skillful touch of the Potter's hand, any usefulness or beauty the clay might have would be destroyed by the pressure and the heat. But Jesus makes suffering understandable to this blob of clay. In the midst of the pressure and the heat, I am confident His hand is on my life, developing my faith until I display His glory, transforming me into a vessel of honor that pleases Him! I don't trust any other potter with my life.

The Vision of His Glory

*To abide
in Christ means
to remain
connected to Him.*

Jesus Is the Source of My Life

"I am the true vine, and my Father is the gardener."

JOHN 15:1

M y husband, Danny, loves to grow things, so we have several pear and apple trees in our yard. Not once have I ever seen one of those fruit trees struggling to bear fruit. Nor do they go to classes or seminars about fruit-bearing or read books about how to be more fruitful. In fact, I don't think those fruit trees ever even think about fruitfulness! Their fruitfulness totally depends on Danny to make sure they get the proper sunlight, water, fertilizer, and pruning.

Jesus taught His disciples about spiritual fruitfulness using a vine, a branch, a gardener, and fruit to illustrate His points.

"I am the vine; you are the branches. If a man remains in me and I in him, he will bear much fruit; apart from me you can do nothing"

JOHN 15:5

For a branch to have fruit-bearing potential, it must be alive. Since it has no life of its own, it must be organically attached to the vine so that the sap, or life, of the vine flows up through the trunk and into the branch.

The branches of a vine "abide" by just remaining connected to the vine. Permanently. Consistently. Day after day, week after week, year after year. They simply rest in their position, allowing the sap of the vine to flow freely through them. They exert no effort of their own. The fruit that is subsequently borne on the branch is actually produced by the life-giving sap within.

To abide in Christ means to remain connected to Him so completely that the "sap" of His Spirit flows through every part of your being, including your mind, will, and emotions as well as your words and deeds. The "fruit" that you then bear is actually produced by His Spirit in you through no conscious effort of your own. If you and I want to be fruitful, we do not concentrate on fruit-bearing; we concentrate on our personal relationship with Jesus Christ.

My Heart's Cry

Jesus ENLARGES MY LIFE

*"He cuts off every branch in me that bears no fruit,
while every branch that does bear fruit
he prunes so that it will be even more fruitful."*

JOHN 15:2

T he abundance of fruit produced by a branch is in
direct proportion to the "size" of the connection
where the branch is joined to the Vine. The smaller
and more constricted the connection, the less fruit is borne
because the capacity for sap is small. The larger and more
expanded the connection, the greater the fruitfulness because
the branch has a greater capacity to be filled with the sap.
In order to expand the connection, the Gardener cuts, clips,
and cleanses the branch to force the connection to the Vine
itself to be enlarged.

There are times when he cuts the branch back so
drastically all that is left of it is the connection to the vine.
Jesus described this drastic pruning in a believer's life when
He explained that the Gardener "cuts off every branch in
me that bears no fruit" (John 15:2).

You and I can trust the Gardener to skillfully, personally,
lovingly, and effectively use the shears in our lives. He will
not cut you back so much that you are broken beyond the
ability to grow, nor will He quench you to the point that
you give up and quit. So trust Him. He's been pruning for
years. He knows what He's doing.

MY HEART'S CRY

49

If we ask anything
according to his will,
he hears us.

1 JOHN 5:14

Jesus Answers—

When I Ask

"I tell you the truth, my Father will give you whatever you ask in my name."

John 16:23

nder close inspection, Jesus' promise contains two prerequisites for receiving answers. The first prerequisite is that you have to ask!

My mother has said that if there are any tears shed in heaven, they are going to be shed over all the answers to prayer for which no one ever bothered to ask!

Why does He wait for us to ask? Maybe He wants us to acknowledge our need of Him. Maybe it's one way of getting our attention. Maybe it's the only way we will know when the answer comes that it comes from Him, and we don't credit ourselves or someone else for it.

Jesus said the second prerequisite is that we must ask in His name.

To pray in Jesus' name means we come to God believing that Jesus is our Lord—believing He has revealed God to us and in response we have submitted to His authority. To pray in Jesus' name means we believe He is our only Savior Whose death on the cross we have claimed personally as atonement for our sin. And it means we acknowledge that He is the Christ, the Messiah, Who has not only come, fulfilling the Law and the Prophets, but He is coming again to reign and rule the world in peace and righteousness.

My Heart's Cry

We have this treasure
in jars of clay to show that
this all-surpassing
power is from God and
is not from us.

2 CORINTHIANS 4:7

 Knows Me

> *Oh LORD, you have searched me and you*
> *know me. You know when I sit and*
> *when I rise; you perceive my thoughts from afar.*
>
> PSALM 139:1–2

W hat a blessed relief to be reminded that Jesus knows me—in fact, He knows me so well He understands that apart from Him I can do nothing.

I don't have to prove myself to Him.

I don't have to worry about disappointing Him.

I don't have to earn His respect.

I don't have to deserve His blessings.

I don't have to work hard to be accepted.

I don't have to produce a quota.

I don't have to be successful.

He created me in the first place. "He knows how [I] am formed, he remembers that [I] am dust" (Psalm 103:14).

JUST GIVE ME JESUS

*The one who
calls you is faithful and
he will do it.*

1 Thessalonians 5:24

Jesus Makes Me Clean

*Wash me thoroughly from my iniquity,
and cleanse me from my sin.*

PSALM 51:2 NKJV

B eside the road leading up to my parents' home in the mountains of western North Carolina is a spring of water. The spring used to flow out of the ground and across the driveway so that part of the road was always wet. In the wintertime, when the temperature dropped below freezing, the water from the spring became a sheet of ice that was hazardous to drivers. So my mother placed an old wooden bucket beside the road, then ran a pipe into the bank of the mountainside where the spring was located. The water from the spring ran through the pipe into the bucket which quickly filled. The overflow from the bucket was channeled into a ditch beside the road so that the hazard of ice was removed.

My mother creatively placed a little tin cup beside the pipe, and on many occasions, as I hiked up that two-mile drive, I would stop for a drink of cold water at the little spring. On occasion, when I came to the bucket, I would find it half-filled with stagnant water. Then I would know something was blocking the pipe. Mother would run a stick through the pipe to dislodge the obstruction. Sometimes it was a small salamander. Sometimes it was a pebble or a dead leaf. But as soon as the obstruction was removed, the water would flow freely once again into the bucket.

Like the spring water, when the Holy Spirit comes into our lives, He fills us with Himself. The only thing that restricts His filling us is our sin. It can be a small, slippery salamander of jealousy or anger or selfishness or worry or lust—just something nasty. It can be a pebble of doubt or pride or bitterness or unforgiveness—something hard. It can be a dead leaf of a memory or a failure or some habit that's unpleasing to God—something flexible and pliable that's hard to pin down. Regardless of what it is, it has to be removed by confessing it so that we might be cleansed and the Water can flow and fruit will be borne.

Jesus addressed the necessity of confronting sin in our lives when He confirmed, "You are already clean because of the word I have spoken to you" (John 15:3). The disciples were already clean because they had placed their faith in Him and given Him their hearts. They continued to be cleansed as they listened to His Word and applied and obeyed it.

In the same way, you and I are clean when we place our faith in Jesus Christ as our Savior Who died on the cross to take away our sin, then give Him our hearts in total surrender. We continue to be cleansed as every day we live by His Word, which we read, apply, and obey. When we sin, we return to the cross by faith, confess it, and ask for cleansing, not so that we might be saved and forgiven, because we are already clean in that sense. We return to the cross for cleansing that we might maintain our fellowship with Christ and the unobstructed flow of the Holy Spirit in our lives.

My Heart's Cry

Jesus Satisfies

*If anyone serves Me, let him follow Me;
and where I am, there My servant will be also.
If anyone serves Me, him My Father will honor.*

John 12:26 nkjv

Are you a Christian who is saved, but not satisfied? Could it be that even though you are assured, through your faith in Christ, that your sins are forgiven and you are going to heaven, you have been living for yourself? Have you left Jesus . . .

> out of your plans?
> out of your activities?
> out of your spare time?
> out of your business?
> out of your decisions?

Has past failure made you shy about including Him in everything? And although you may be very busy, are you still coming up empty on the inside? There is a richness and depth of satisfaction reserved for those who not only know Jesus as their Savior but also totally live for Him as their Lord.

When you and I serve Jesus in His way, according to His will, in obedience to His Word, for His glory and kingdom alone, we are satisfied! Others may be blessed through our service but not any more than we ourselves are blessed.

Just Give Me Jesus

The Christian life is motivated, not by a list of do's and don'ts, but by the gracious outpouring of God's love and blessing.

Jesus SHOWERS ME
WITH BLESSINGS

Blessings are on the head of the righteous.

PROVERBS 10:6 NKJV

egardless of our past failures or present shortcomings, our relationship with Jesus Christ ensures that "from the fullness of his grace we have all received one blessing after another" (John 1:16).

When the Mediterranean Sea evaporates or runs low, the Atlantic Ocean rushes in at the Strait of Gibraltar to replenish it and keep it full. When you and I are related to Jesus Christ, our strength and wisdom and peace and joy and love and hope may run out, but His life rushes in to keep us filled to the brim—not because of anything we have or have not done, but just because of Him we are showered with blessings.

That's the fullness of His grace. We don't deserve it. We can't earn it. We can't bargain for it. We can't buy it. We just open our hearts and hands to receive it. One blessing after another blessing after another blessing. For a lifetime! Forever!

JUST GIVE ME JESUS

It is he who made us,
and we are his; . . .
the sheep of his pasture.

PSALM 100:3

Jesus CARES ABOUT ME

When Jesus landed and saw
a large crowd, he had compassion on them.

MARK 6:34

J esus saw people not as an interruption, but as an opportunity to reveal His loving care and His Father's compassionate power to meet their deepest needs.

Jesus saw people as sheep who needed a shepherd.

He saw people as God saw them.

Jesus cares about your job, about whether your child makes the sports team, about your children's college tuition, about your budget now that you are unexpectedly pregnant, about the roof that leaks, about the cranky transmission in the car, and about all the other physical problems and needs we face.

Jesus cares even if the physical problem we face is largely of our own making. He cares if we are having car trouble, even if it was caused by our not having taken the time to change the oil regularly. He cares if we are having financial struggles, even if they were caused by our having run up massive debts on our charge accounts for things we wanted but did not necessarily need. Jesus cares about your physical needs today.

JUST GIVE ME JESUS

"*Father forgive them*
for they do not
know what they do."

Luke 23:34 NKJV

Jesus Helps Me
Forgive Others

*Be kind to one another, tenderhearted,
forgiving one another, even as God in Christ forgave you.*

Ephesians 4:32 NKJV

I f Jesus forgave those who nailed Him to the Cross, and if God forgives you and me, how can you withhold your forgiveness from someone else? How can you withhold your forgiveness from yourself? If God says, "I forgive you," who are you to say, "Thank You, God, but I can't forgive myself"? Are your standards higher than His? Are you more righteous than He is? If God says, "I forgive you," then the only appropriate response is to say, "God, thank You. I don't deserve it, but I accept it. And to express my gratitude, I, in turn, forgive that person who has sinned against me."

We forgive others, not because they deserve it, but because He deserves it! The only reason we have to forgive is that He commands us to, and our obedience gives us opportunity to say to Him, "Thank You for forgiving me. I love You." Our forgiveness of others then becomes an act of worship that we would not enter into except for Who He is and for the overwhelming debt of love we owe Him.

JUST GIVE ME JESUS

May our
Lord Jesus Christ
himself . . . encourage
your hearts.

2 Thessalonians 2:16–17

Jesus Makes a Little Bit, Enough

> *Jesus then took the loaves, gave thanks,*
> *and distributed to those who were seated as much as*
> *they wanted. He did the same with the fish.*
>
> JOHN 6:11

One day long ago Jesus and His disciples had slipped into the hill country hoping for a time of retreat. Instead, five thousand people showed up, wanting Jesus to heal and teach them—which He graciously did. None of the five thousand had eaten all day long—and most had not brought any provision for a meal.

The disciples wanted to send them away since they had no food, either. But Jesus told His disciples to feed them— an impossible task. However, Andrew was resourceful enough to find a little boy with five loaves and two fish—which seemed totally inadequate for the need at hand. And it was totally inadequate! That little bit of food was less than nothing when compared to more than five thousand hungry people! But it was all the little boy and the disciples had to give. Jesus took it, and blessed it, and broke it, and handed it back to the disciples—and they passed it out, and continued passing it out, until all five thousand people were fed to the full!

The point Jesus got across to His disciples was that it didn't matter if they only had a little bit—a little bit . . .

of time,

of money,

of education,

of ability,
of knowledge,
of strength,
of resources . . .
what mattered was that they gave all that they had to Jesus.
Then He would make it enough.

MY HEART'S CRY

Jesus GIVES ME HIS
UNDIVIDED ATTENTION

"I am with you always, even to the end of the age."

MATTHEW 28:20

O n the very same night Jesus was betrayed, within twelve hours of His crucifixion, when the horror of the impending accusations, rejection, torture, and humiliation must have begun to settle on Him like a smothering cloak, His thoughts centered not on His own impending suffering but on His disciples' grief over His departure! As He prepared to go to the cross, with selfless abandonment He sought to comfort His disciples in their grief and loneliness! He began to patiently explain that His presence would remain with them, but He would no longer be visible. He would be invisible in the person of the Holy Spirit.

Do you long for—even dream of—someone who would understand you to such depth that he would know what you were thinking and what you were feeling without your having to say a word? Someone who would tenderly look into your eyes and you would know that he knew—everything!

Then you need Jesus—because He knows you, He understands you, and you have His undivided attention.

The Holy Spirit is Jesus in me—
giving all of Himself to me—
with undivided attention!
Always!

MY HEART'S CRY

*God never expects
more from me
than the Holy Spirit
would do in
and through me.*

Jesus Gives Me
THE COMFORTER

> *"It is expedient for you that I go away: for if I*
> *go not away, the Comforter will not come unto you;*
> *but if I depart, I will send him unto you."*
>
> JOHN 16:7 KJV

T his very promise Jesus gave us contains a name for the Holy Spirit that reveals the uniqueness of His nearness in our lives. This name, "Comforter," is equally translated from the Greek text into six other names, each of which describes a slightly different aspect of the Holy Spirit's precious, personal ministry in our lives:

Comforter: One who relieves another of mental distress.

Counselor: One whose profession is to give advice and manage causes.

Helper: One who furnishes with relief or support.

Intercessor: One who acts between parties to reconcile differences.

Advocate: One who pleads the cause of another.

Strengthener: One who causes you to become stronger, endure, and resist attacks.

Standby: One who can be relied upon either for regular use or in emergencies.

Can you imagine how wonderful it would be to have Someone with these attributes in your life?

MY HEART'S CRY

"When he, the Spirit
of truth, comes,
he will guide you into all truth.
He will not speak on his own;
he will speak only what he hears,
and he will tell you
what is yet to come."

JOHN 16:13

Jesus OPENS MY MIND
TO HIS WORD

He opened their minds
so they could understand the Scriptures.

LUKE 24:45

T he Bible is a wonderful book of history and poetry and prophecy and ceremony. Anyone can be blessed by just reading this truly magnificent piece of literature that spans the years of human history. But there is a unique blessing that is reserved for those who prayerfully, earnestly, and humbly approach it by faith as the truth, seeking to go past the surface reading into the deeper meaning. And it is impossible to reach this deeper level of understanding and blessing without the Holy Spirit's guidance.

As you and I seek to read and study, understand and apply, submit to and obey the Bible, we are not alone. The Holy Spirit gives clarity to the wonderful Book He has inspired. Again and again I have sat at my desk, staring at the Scripture passage I have just read and doodling with the pen on my legal pad because my mind has gone blank. It's as though I know what the passage says in words, but the meaning of the passage for my life totally escapes me. Then I pray and ask the Holy Spirit to unlock the meaning for me, and as I continue to meditate, a thought will come . . . then another thought . . . until the passage opens up and I can see the treasure that's on the inside.

MY HEART'S CRY

PART THREE

Jesus

IS THE SHEPHERD
WHO GUIDES US

We are drawn to
the unconditional nature
of God's love.

Jesus REVEALS
GOD'S LOVE

This is how God showed his love among us:
He sent his one and only Son into the world that
we might live through him.

1 JOHN 4:9

B efore the foundation of the world was laid, God, in His divine sovereignty, planned to send His own Son to the cross to be our Savior. Before the beginning of time and space and human history, He took counsel with Himself and decided to bring us into existence, knowing full well that we would rebel against Him and become separated from Him by our sin. So He made preparations for our redemption—preparations that were finished once and for all time at the cross.

The heartbeat of Jesus was to finish His Father's plan and, in so doing, bring glory to God. In other words, through His own death on the cross, Jesus would reveal the love of God in such a way that people throughout the ages would praise Him and love Him and lay down their lives before Him. So He embraced the cross and all that it meant.

MY HEART'S CRY

Thanks be to God
for his
indescribable gift!

2 Corinthians 9:15

Jesus Is God in the Flesh

> *He came and preached peace to you*
> *who were afar off and to those who were near.*
>
> EPHESIANS 2:17 NKJV

ithout the Holy Spirit to clarify the truth to our minds and confirm Who Jesus is in our hearts, we would "see" Jesus as just . . .

a man,

or a holy man,

or a prophet,

or a great prophet,

or a teacher,

or a revolutionary,

or a religious icon,

or a symbolic figure!

But the Holy Spirit opens our eyes to see and our minds to know and our hearts to receive that Jesus is . . .

the Messiah of Israel,

the Lamb of God,

the Son of Man,

the Savior of the world,

the Truth incarnate,

the risen Lord,

the reigning King . . .

God Himself in the flesh!

MY HEART'S CRY

*I live by faith
in the Son of God,
who loved me and gave
himself for me.*

GALATIANS 2:20

Jesus Does Care

Greater love has no one than this,
than to lay down one's life for his friends.

JOHN 15:13 NKJV

W hen have you felt so totally helpless that your prayer was fathoms deeper than mere words—it was a desperate heart's cry? Was it when some bad thing happened to someone you love? Was it when you experienced . . .

a physical illness?

a financial collapse?

a severed relationship?

a social rejection?

a family betrayal?

an emotional abuse?

Did you think because something bad happened, it indicated Jesus doesn't really know what's going on? Or that maybe He knows, but He's not pleased with you? Or that *if* He does know, He just doesn't love you or your family enough to do anything about it? Are you interpreting His love *by your circumstances* instead of interpreting your circumstances *by His love?* When we are tempted to question whether or not He cares, we are reminded that, "While we were still sinners, Christ died for us" (Romans 5:8). *He does care!*

WHY? TRUSTING GOD WHEN YOU DON'T UNDERSTAND

Trust Jesus
to know best.

Jesus IS TRUSTWORTHY

I trust in your unfailing love;
my heart rejoices in your salvation.

PSALM 13:5 NKJV

J esus is not offended by our ignorance or our confusion or our questions. On the contrary, He knows exactly what we are thinking and feeling, and He takes the initiative to help us understand.

At times, when our understanding is limited, we simply have to trust Him to know best. We have to trust His silences and respect His mysteries and wait for His answers.

When we pray for the salvation of a friend, and she becomes more hostile . . .

When we pray for the healing of a loved one, and he dies . . .

When we pray for release from a financial burden, and we go bankrupt . . .

When we pray for a reconciliation, and we are handed divorce papers . . .

When we pray for our career, and we get laid off . . .

When we pray for protection, and we are robbed . . .

When we pray for the purity of an unmarried daughter, and she becomes pregnant . . .

We just have to trust Him. Trust Him. Trust Him!

We serve a living Lord Who loves to answer the prayers of His children. Be patient! Trust Him to know best.

MY HEART'S CRY

He Himself has said,
"I will never leave you
nor forsake you."

HEBREWS 13:5 NKJV

Jesus Is Everywhere

> *Neither death nor life, nor angels nor principalities*
> *nor powers, nor things present nor things to come, nor height*
> *nor depth, nor any other created thing, shall be able to separate*
> *us from the love of God which is in Christ Jesus our Lord.*
>
> ROMANS 8:38–39 NKJV

Y ou and I can be where Jesus is—now, and for all eternity—because He lives within us and has promised that He will never leave us nor forsake us!

When your parents forsake you through death or abandonment, or your spouse forsakes you through divorce, you have His presence. (Psalm 27:10)

When the fire of adversity increases in intensity, you have His presence. (Daniel 9:1–25)

When you are overwhelmed by burdens or depression, you have His presence. (Isaiah 43:2)

When you and I follow Jesus, He promises that we will be where He is. And there is not one place in the entire universe, visible or invisible, where He is not! Jesus is everywhere!

MY HEART'S CRY

*The God of
all grace . . . will . . .
make you strong,
firm, and steadfast.*

1 PETER 5:10

Jesus Is with Me in Suffering

When you pass through the waters, I will be with you.

ISAIAH 43:2

Have your thoughts been similar to these?

God, where have You been? Why did You let this happen? I just don't understand.

Are you overlooking the fact that Jesus has drawn near to you?

Are you blinded to His presence by your own tears?

Are you deafened to His gentle voice by your own accusations?

While He doesn't always protect those He loves from suffering or answer our prayers the way we ask Him to, He does promise in His Word that He will be present with us in the midst of our suffering and pain.

The apostle John, suffering in exile on Patmos near the end of his life, must have prayed earnestly to be restored to his church and to his ministry. He must have begged God to get him off of the remote island so he could continue preaching and serving as a pastor and evangelist. Yet God didn't answer his prayers. Instead, John related that it was on Patmos that God drew near to him and gave him a vision of the glory of Jesus Christ—a vision he recorded for the encouragement of every generation of believers since that time in the Book of Revelation. Jesus was with John in exile on Patmos!

WHY? TRUSTING GOD WHEN YOU DON'T UNDERSTAND

My God will meet
all your needs according
to his glorious riches
in Christ Jesus.

Jesus IS MY SHEPHERD

My sheep hear My voice,
and I know them, and they follow Me.

JOHN 10:27 NKJV

The Eastern shepherd of Jesus' day raised his sheep primarily in the Judean uplands. The countryside was rocky, hilly, and creased with deep crevices and ravines. Patches of grass were sparse. So the shepherd had to establish a personal relationship with each sheep, nurturing its love and trust in him in order to lead it to where the path was the smoothest, the grass was the greenest, the water was the cleanest, and the nights were the safest. The shepherd always led the sheep. He knew their names, and when he called them, they recognized his voice, following him like a swarm of little chicks follows the mother hen. When he stopped, the sheep huddled closely around him, pressing against his legs. Their personal relationship with him was based on his voice, which they knew and trusted.

The Bible describes our relationship with Jesus as being similar to the relationship between the Eastern shepherd and his sheep—a relationship based on His voice. And make no mistake about it, His voice is God's Word, the Holy Bible.

When I tend to be afraid, I just fall back on Who God is and rest in Him. He cannot be less than Himself! And my God is God! He is the God of gods Who has made Himself visible and knowable and approachable through Jesus Christ—which is why Jesus commanded us to "trust also" in Him.

MY HEART'S CRY

Soaring with God
is an adventure
of discovering
just how faithful
He can be.

Jesus Helps Me Soar

*[Jesus] got up, rebuked the wind and
said to the waves, "Quiet! Be still!" Then the wind
died down and it was completely calm.*

MARK 4:39

A turkey and an eagle react differently to the threat of a storm. A turkey reacts by running under the barn, hoping the storm won't come near. On the other hand, an eagle leaves the security of its nest and spreads its wings to ride the air currents of the approaching storm, knowing they will carry it higher in the sky than it could soar on its own.

When the storms of life threaten, it's natural for me to be a turkey in my emotions, but I have chosen to be an eagle in my spirit. And as I have spread my wings of faith to embrace the "Wind," placing my trust in Jesus and Jesus alone, I have experienced quiet, "everyday" miracles:

His grace has been more than adequate to cover me.
His power has lifted my burden.
His peace has calmed my worries.
His joy has balanced my pain.
His strength has been sufficient to carry me through.
His love has bathed my wounds like a healing balm.

WHY? TRUSTING GOD WHEN YOU DON'T UNDERSTAND

He saved us,
not because of
righteous things we
had done, but because
of his mercy.

TITUS 3:5

Jesus ANSWERS PRAYER

*"If you abide in Me and My words
abide in you, you will ask what you desire,
and it shall be done for you.*

JOHN 15:7 NKJV

L ike any effective communication, prayer should be
two-sided. It involves our asking and also our
listening. In other words, prayer is a conversation.
We speak to Jesus in prayer then listen attentively as He
speaks to us through His Word. Effective communication
that gets results always involves our Bibles, something that
Jesus emphasized when He explained, "If you [abide] in me
and my words [abide] in you, ask whatever you wish, and it
will be given you" (John 15:7). What are your wishes?
Do you wish for . . .

a spouse?

a child?

a car?

a house?

good health?

more money?

more friends?

a better job?

a longer life?

fame?

popularity?

Do you think the promise that Jesus gave His disciples
was like handing them a Divine Genie in a bottle? And that

if they would just rub the bottle with enough faith, the Genie would pop out and grant them their "wishes"?

As ludicrous as that is, it actually is the way some people view prayer. And when the Genie doesn't pop out of the bottle, they become offended with God and resent Him for not being at their beck and call.

One major prerequisite to receiving answers to prayer is that our requests line up with God's will. And the only way we will know what God's will is, is if we are abiding consistently in His Word. Instead of basing our prayers on "I hope so," our prayers are based on "God says so." And if we are saturating ourselves in His Word, then His desires will be ours, which then become the prayers of our heart.

MY HEART'S CRY

Jesus GUARANTEES IMMEDIATE ACCESS TO GOD

Let us therefore come boldly to the throne of grace, that we may obtain mercy and find grace to help in time of need.

HEBREWS 4:16 NKJV

T he only credentials that God accepts are those presented to Him in the name and righteousness of His dear Son. So pray—in Jesus' name. It's your privilege as the Father's child!

When you approach God through faith in His Son, God is accessible twenty-four hours a day, seven days a week, twelve months a year for the rest of your life!

For the last several years, I have carried a small cellular phone with me whenever I leave the house. Even when I take my early morning, three-mile walk, I have my cell phone in my pocket. Invariably, when I say good-bye to my husband, or speak with my children or staff before I go out of town, I remind them that I will have my phone with me. If I'm needed, all they have to do is call me. Yet how many times have I noticed that I have a voice message waiting on my phone because either it was out of the range of a tower, or I had turned it off while flying, or muted it during a meeting, or left it in that other pocketbook!

Praise God! He is never out of range! He is never turned off or tuned out! His ears are never deaf! He is always available, accessible, and attentive to our call!

MY HEART'S CRY

*"Do not let your
hearts be troubled.
Trust in God;
trust also in me."*

JOHN 14:1

Jesus Is God's
Ultimate Answer

When you pass through the waters,
I will be with you; and through the rivers,
they shall not overflow you.

Isaiah 43:2 NKJV

To our heart-wrenched cries of Why? God's ultimate answer is, "Jesus," as He is glorified and magnified in our lives through our suffering. Trust Him. When guilt takes the edge off every joy . . .

when there are no answers to your questions . . .
When you don't understand why, just trust Him!
Trust His heart.
Trust His purpose!
Trust His goodness!
Trust Him to know best.
Trust His plan to be bigger than yours!
Trust Him to keep His Word.
Trust Him—and Him alone.

Why? Trusting God When You Don't Understand

Greater love
has no one than this,
that he lay down his life
for his friends.

John 15:13

Jesus Is My
Personal Friend

"You are my friends if you do what I command."

John 15:14

What could be a greater privilege than to have Jesus call us His friend? If I told you that the president of the United States was my friend, you would probably snicker. And rightly so. Although I have briefly met him, I don't really know him, and any "friendship" is based on what I have read about him. But if the president of the United States stated that, "Anne Lotz is my friend," it would be impressive. It would indicate a relationship based on personal knowledge that he publicly affirmed.

Jesus did more than say you and I could call Him our friend. He promises He will call us His friends! Now that's impressive! That's a privileged position! Do you struggle with an inferiority complex? Then hold your head a little higher because when you choose to abide in Christ and obey His command to love others sacrificially,

the Son of God,

the Savior of the world,

the sovereign Lord,

the sweet Rose of Sharon,

the Lord of glory,

the King of Kings and Lord of Lords,

the most important Man in all of the universe,

counts you as His personal friend!

My Heart's Cry

My help
comes from the LORD,
the Maker of
heaven and earth.

PSALM 121:2

Jesus WEEPS WITH ME

> *"In this world you will have trouble.*
> *But take heart! I have overcome the world."*
>
> JOHN 16:33

W hile Jesus was in the Trans-Jordan He received the urgent message that Lazarus, His beloved friend, was sick. He decided to go to Bethany, where Lazarus and his family lived.

After delaying his journey for two days, Jesus left the Trans-Jordan, walking all day on rocky roads over hills turned brown by the heat. Finally, He and His disciples came to the little village of Bethany that He had come to love. As soon as He drew near, He was greeted with the tragic news—of which He was already aware—that Lazarus had died.

That day in Bethany, as Mary wept and her friends wept with her, a tumult of grief and anger and compassion and empathy welled up within the heart of Jesus until He could no longer contain His feelings. In a voice that must have been choking with emotion, He inquired, "Where have you laid him?" When those around Him replied gently, "'Come and see, Lord.' . . . Jesus wept" (John 11:34–35).

Jesus, the Creator of the universe, the eternal I Am, so strong, so powerful, so wise, so human, stood there with tears running down His cheeks! He knew He intended to raise Lazarus from the dead, but still He wept. Why? Because He loved Mary and Martha and Lazarus, and their tears of grief were on His face!

When have you grieved at the grave of a loved one,
or trembled from the shock of discovering the
     pregnancy of your unmarried daughter,
or recoiled at the diagnosis of a doctor,
or walked through the nightmare of a precinct station
     to face your child's arrest,
or felt the cold, numb shock of early dismissal from
     your job,
or experienced the searing pain of a spouse's betrayal?
Did you think Jesus just didn't care? That if God really
loved you, He would have intervened to prevent it? All
those thoughts crowding into your mind are like seeds sown
by the Enemy. If you are not alert, those seeds will grow up
into weeds that choke out and strangle the truth—that God
so loves you, your grief is His, your nightmare is His, your
shock is His, your pain is His. Your tears are on His face!

My Heart's Cry

Jesus Empowers Me

> *"When the Counselor comes, whom I will send to you from the Father, the Spirit of truth who goes out from the Father, he will testify about me."*
>
> <small>John 15:26</small>

T he source of power that filled Jesus, enabling Him to face His accusers and His execution with dignified compassion and courageous strength, is the same source of power that enabled the disciples to live and die for Jesus. And it's the same source of power available to you and me today!

When have you spoken up for Jesus? When have you told someone about Jesus who doesn't know Him? Are you recoiling in fear, protesting, "Anne, I could never do that! I'm afraid my neighbors would never speak to me again. I'm afraid my friends will laugh at me or be derisive about something that's precious to me. I'm afraid to speak up for Jesus because I may lose my popularity or promotion or position or prestige or possessions or . . ."

Jesus understands your fears. That's why He has sent you and me the Holy Spirit. When we open our mouths, the Holy Spirit not only gives us words, He clothes the words with power to make a difference in the hearer. But we need to open our mouths!

<small>My Heart's Cry</small>

God has poured out
his love
into our hearts by
the Holy Spirit.

ROMANS 5:5

Jesus Fills Me with God's Love

God has poured out his love into our hearts by
the Holy Spirit, whom he has given us.

ROMANS 5:5

D id you know that you are God's special loved one? Why would He love you so? Maybe it's because when you abide in Christ you are so saturated in Jesus that when God looks at you, He sees His own precious Son and envelopes you in His love for Jesus' sake!

As you and I develop and grow in this love relationship with God, abiding with Him through meaningful prayer and Bible reading, getting to know Him on a deeper level as we live out what we say we believe, He fills us with Himself. And "God is love" (1 John 4:16). As you and I are filled with God, we will be filled with His love, not only for Himself, but for others—which includes our spouses or the incompatible people with whom we are struggling. God has promised to pour out "his love into our hearts by the Holy Spirit, whom he has given us" (Romans 5:5).

MY HEART'S CRY

*Nothing is impossible
with God.*

LUKE 1:37

Jesus DEFEATS FEAR

> *There is no fear in love; but perfect love casts*
> *out fear, because fear involves torment.*
> *But he who fears has not been made perfect in love.*

1 JOHN 4:18 NKJV

D o not let your hearts be troubled" (John 14:1) is a command you and I are to obey! Deliberately calming ourselves is a choice we are to make in the face of shocking setbacks,

catastrophic circumstances,

abrupt accidents,

irritating interruptions,

devastating dissension,

agonizing addiction,

frequent failures,

all of which cause us to be terrified of the consequences and repercussions. In the midst of the swirling, cloying fog of fear, Jesus commands, "Stop it!"

Stop letting your imagination run wild.

Stop analyzing every detail over and over again.

Stop flogging yourself with the "if only's" and "what if's."

Stop being afraid!

How in the world is it possible to obey a command that involves so much of our emotional feelings? Our obedience begins with a choice to stop being afraid, followed by a decision to start trusting God.

MY HEART'S CRY

105

The Lord is the strength of my life; of whom shall I be afraid?

PSALM 27:1 NKJV

Jesus Is My
ANTIDOTE TO FEAR

I sought the LORD, and he answered me;
he delivered me from all my fears.

PSALM 34:4

T he antidote to fear is faith.

When I toss and turn in the middle of the night, worried and fearful over something that is impending in my life or the life of someone I love, I am comforted and calmed as I meditate on Who God is. It helps me plant my faith in Someone Who is bigger than my fears, because He is . . .

Able (2 TIMOTHY 1:12)

Benevolent (EPHESIANS 1:3)

Compassionate (PSALM 145:8)

Dependable (PSALM 119:138)

Eternal (DEUTERONOMY 33:27)

Faithful (LAMENTATIONS 3:23)

Good (PSALM 73:1)

Holy (1 PETER 1:16)

Immortal (1 TIMOTHY 1:17)

Just (2 THESSALONIANS 1:6)

Kind (JEREMIAH 9:24)

Loving (1 JOHN 4:16)

Merciful (DANIEL 9:8)

Near (PHILIPPIANS 4:5)

Omniscient (LUKE 9:47)

Powerful (NUMBERS 14:13)

Quick (DEUTERONOMY 33:26)

Right (EZRA 9:15)

Sufficient (2 CORINTHIANS 3:5)

Truthful (JOHN 3:33)

Unique (PSALM 72:18)

Victorious (1 CORINTHIANS 15:57)

Wise (ROMANS 16:27)

XYZalted! (PSALM 92:8)

And God is fully revealed in Jesus! "He is the image of the invisible God. . ." (Colossians 1:15).

JUST GIVE ME JESUS

PART FOUR

Jesus

IS THE ETERNAL KING
WHO LOVES US

God is love.
Whoever lives in love
lives in God,
and God in him.

1 JOHN 4:16

Jesus LOVES ME

This is how we know what love is:
Jesus Christ laid down his life for us.

J esus so loves us, that when His Father sent Him to earth to die as a sacrifice for our sin, He came. He confined Himself to a woman's womb for nine months, then submitted to the human birth process. He limited Himself to the body of a two-year-old and then subjected Himself to the changes of adolescence, growing in wisdom and stature and favor with God and man. At the age of thirty-three He willingly died on the cross, being obedient even unto death. He was buried in a borrowed tomb, then on the third day rose up from the dead. He ascended into heaven, where He sits at the right hand of the Father, ever living to make intercession for you and me. He has asked the Father to send down His Holy Spirit to indwell those who receive Him by faith. And one day, He will return to rule the world in peace and righteousness and justice! The Bible says He is Savior, Lord, and King.

MY HEART'S CRY

When you have
done the will of God,
you will receive what he
has promised.

HEBREWS 10:36

*When you have
done the will of God,
you will receive what he
has promised.*

Hebrews 10:36

 IS FULLY

PRESENT WITH ME

May the Lord of peace Himself give you
peace always in every way. The Lord be with you all.

2 THESSALONIANS 3:16 NKJV

J esus is eternally omnipresent. He always has been, always is, always will be. He is eternally the same yesterday, today, and forever. He did not undergo some radical personality change when He came to earth. He is the same today as He was at creation, as He will be when He reigns on the earth. He is fully present in every age, every generation, every culture, every nation.

His omnipresence brings comfort because I am assured He is fully present with me even as I write this at my desk at home. He is fully present with my children living in different cities and states. He is fully present with my husband at work. Being everywhere at once does not deplete or dilute His Person or His power in any way. Jesus Christ is all-powerful, fully in charge.

THE VISION OF HIS GLORY

No one,
nor anything,
is mightier than Jesus!

Jesus Loves Me

> *This is how we know what love is:*
> *Jesus Christ laid down his life for us.*
>
> 1 John 3:16

Jesus so loves us, that when His Father sent Him to earth to die as a sacrifice for our sin, He came. He confined Himself to a woman's womb for nine months, then submitted to the human birth process. He limited Himself to the body of a two-year-old and then subjected Himself to the changes of adolescence, growing in wisdom and stature and favor with God and man. At the age of thirty-three He willingly died on the cross, being obedient even unto death. He was buried in a borrowed tomb, then on the third day rose up from the dead. He ascended into heaven, where He sits at the right hand of the Father, ever living to make intercession for you and me. He has asked the Father to send down His Holy Spirit to indwell those who receive Him by faith. And one day, He will return to rule the world in peace and righteousness and justice! The Bible says He is Savior, Lord, and King.

My Heart's Cry

Jesus REWARDS ME

> *The Son of Man will come in the glory*
> *of His Father with His angels, and then He will*
> *reward each according to his works.*
>
> MATTHEW 16:27 NKJV

All through the Bible, we are encouraged and exhorted, commanded and compelled, to be faithful in life and in service. Jesus said repeatedly that we are to do our "acts of righteousness" so that our Father, "who sees what is done in secret, will reward you" (Matt. 6:1, 4).

My children were always expected to do their share of the housework when growing up. But on those occasions when I did more thorough cleaning, in order to motivate them to wash windows or clean out closets and drawers or polish silver, I offered them the reward of cash. It was amazing to see the difference the promise of a reward made, not only in their attitude, but in the quality of their work! They were much more pleasant in their attitude and much more conscientious in their tasks.

The same is true in the Christian life. The promise of a reward adds eagerness to our attitude and energy to our work. It changes our motivation from "I have to do this" to "I want to do this." It may be the reward of God's pleasure that motivates us, or the reward of a crown to lay at His feet, or perhaps the reward of a position of authority in His earthly kingdom.

THE VISION OF HIS GLORY

"I know the plans
I have for you,"
declares the LORD, "plans
to prosper you and not to
harm you, plans to give
you hope and a future."

JEREMIAH 29:11

Jesus Promises Me Eternal Life

*No eye has seen, no ear has heard, no mind
has conceived what God has prepared for those who love him.*

1 Corinthians 2:9

T hrough faith in Jesus Christ, anyone and everyone can live forever!

Within the past year, I had the opportunity once again to visit Westminster Abbey in London. It is a grand cathedral where many of the kings and dignitaries of England are buried, and where the kings and queens receive their coronation. The narthex is small, dark, and cramped—just a brief space to pass through between the outside door and the door leading into the cathedral itself. I can't imagine anyone visiting the abbey and being satisfied to stay in the narthex. I also can't imagine anyone who would make an enormous effort to stay there with no thought to passing through to the glory of what lies beyond.

Your life and mine here on earth is like the narthex to a grand cathedral. Our lives are simply an area to pass through on our way to the glory of eternal life that lies beyond the door of death. Physical death for a believer is simply a transition into real life. And it's God's purpose that you and I live forever—with Him.

My Heart's Cry

117

The LORD will
fulfill his purpose
for me.

PSALM 138:8

Jesus Will Honor Me

"Whoever serves me must follow me;
and where I am, my servant also will be.
My Father will honor the one who serves me."

JOHN 12:26

hen Jesus says we will be with Him where He is, where will He be? He will be in heaven, at the Father's right hand! The disciples had been disappointed that they would not rule with Jesus in an earthly kingdom, yet here He was promising them a place of honor in a universal kingdom!

If for no other reason, because of our love for His Son,

our obedience to His Son,

our faith in His Son,

and our service to His Son,

the Father loves us, accepts us, takes pleasure in us, and will one day honor us.

MY HEART'S CRY

*We, according to
His promise, look for
new heavens and a new
earth in which
righteousness dwells.*

2 PETER 3:13 NKJV

Jesus Is Preparing
Heaven for Me

In my Father's house are many rooms; if it were not so,
I would have told you. I am going there to prepare a place
for you. And if I go and prepare a place for you,
I will come back and take you to be with me
that you also may be where I am.

John 14:2–3

he Creator Who created all the earthly beauty we
have grown to love—
      The majestic snow-capped peaks of the Alps,
The rushing mountain streams,
The brilliantly colored fall leaves,
The carpets of wildflowers,
The glistening fin of a fish as it leaps out of a sparkling sea,
The graceful gliding of a swan across the lake,
The lilting notes of a canary's song,
The whir of a hummingbird's wings,
The shimmer of the dew on the grass in early morning,
    This is the same Creator Who has prepared our
heavenly home for us! If God could make the heavens and
earth as beautiful as we think they are today—which
includes thousands of years of wear and tear, corruption and
pollution, sin and selfishness—can you imagine what the
new heaven and new earth will look like? It will be much
more glorious than any eyes have seen, any ears have heard,
or any minds have ever conceived!

Regardless of your present . . .
circumstances or crisis,
pressures or pain,
suffering or sorrow,
failures or frustrations,
danger or disease,
memories or misery,
temptations or trials,
problems or persecutions,
burdens or brokenness,

your situation is temporary compared to eternity. And
eternity is going to be spent with Jesus in His Father's house
that has been lovingly prepared just for you! That's the truth!
Your future has been confirmed!

My Heart's Cry

Jesus Will Take Me Home

*Yea, though I walk through the valley
of the shadow of death, I will fear no evil;
for You are with me; Your rod and
Your staff, they comfort me.*

PSALM 23:4 NKJV

W hen my husband's mother walked into a room, it was as though the lights came on. She had such a vivacious, happy, energetic disposition that the sun still seemed to shine in her presence even on a gloomy day. Gramma, as we affectionately called her, not only raised four strapping sons who adored her, she was also the "first lady" of the churches pastored by her husband. She sang in the choir, supervised the church suppers, led women's Bible studies, visited the sick and infirm, and cared for the helpless. And until she was seventy-five years old, she worked as a dental hygienist on Fifth Avenue in New York City. Yet she never did learn to drive a car!

One morning when she was eighty-one years of age, she and Grampa were on their usual outing when Grampa ran off the road and hit a telephone pole. Although he was just shaken up, Gramma was critically injured. Six weeks later it seemed as though she would make a full recovery and be able to come home from the hospital.

At six o'clock in the morning on the day before she was to go home, she called my husband. She vividly described what she said had been a dream in which she had walked

The Lord will . . .
preserve me for
His heavenly kingdom.

2 TIMOTHY 4:18 NKJV

along a beach. The cloudless sky was crystal blue, and the sand had been soft beneath her feet, and the waves had rolled gently into shore, and Jesus had been walking with her, holding her hand! She hung up the phone, and an hour later we received the call that she had gone to His Father's house!

Once in a while we are given a glimpse of the fulfillment of our Lord's promise that confirms our future. At the moment of death, Jesus comes personally to take His children to His Father's house!

My Heart's Cry

ACKNOWLEDGMENTS

Grateful acknowledgment is made to the following publisher for permission to reprint the enclosed material from these published works of Anne Graham Lotz:

The Vision of His Glory (Nashville: W Publishing Group,1996).

Just Give me Jesus (Nashville: W Publishing Group, 2000).

Why? Trusting God When You Don't Understand (Nashville: W Publishing, 2001).

My Heart's Cry (Nashville: W Publishing, 2002).

Other titles available from Anne Graham Lotz
Daily Light Devotional (Nashville: J Countryman, 1998)
Daily Light Journal (Nashville: J Countryman, 1999)
Heaven: My Father's House (Nashville: W Publishing, 2001)
The Joy of My Heart (Nashville: W Publishing, 2004)
My Jesus Is Everything (Nashville: J Countryman, 2005)
I Saw the Lord (Grand Rapids: Zondervan, 2006)